# The do-it-yourself Guide to... Age Defiance

*by Marianne Richmond*

# The do-it-yourself Guide to...
# Age Defiance

© 2004 by Marianne Richmond Studios, Inc.

All rights reserved. No part of this book may be reproduced or transmitted in any form or by any means, electronic or mechanical, including photocopying, recording or any information storage and retrieval system, without permission in writing from the publisher.

Marianne Richmond Studios, Inc.
420 N. 5th Street, Suite 840
Minneapolis, MN 55401
www.mariannerichmond.com

ISBN 0-9753528-5-7

Illustrations by Marianne Richmond

Book design by Sara Dare Biscan

Printed in China

Second Printing

How do you feel about aging?
   Yes, we know.


We run, but we can't hide.
   We exfoliate, highlight, hydrate, detoxify, slim down, tone up, inject, and correct... all in an effort to outsmart the effects of time!


   Why didn't someone tell us that baby oil and tin foil was a bad, bad idea?

Well, girlfriend — cheer <u>up</u>!
 We have created just for you...

The do-it-yourself Guide to
 Age Defiance... a practical collection
of home remedies for the
 youth-seeker in all of us.

And the good news?
 They're inexpensive... and as accessible
as your laundry room or basement!

wrinkles

graying hair

rough skin texture

incontinence

thinning eyebrows

*sagging breasts*

enlarged pores

*thinning lips*

age spots

flabby tummy

*cellulite*

*wiggly neck*

# Hot Flashes!

drooping eyelids

sluggish libido

And should you still not get

the results you want?

deal!

A gifted author and artist, Marianne Richmond shares her creations with millions of people worldwide through her delightful books, cards, and giftware. In addition to the *Simply Said...* and *Smartly Said...* gift book series, she has written and illustrated five additional books: **The Gift of an Angel, The Gift of a Memory, Hooray for You!, The Gifts of Being Grand,** and **I Love You So....**

To learn more about Marianne's products, please visit www.mariannerichmond.com.